VIRTUAL REALITY

VIRTUAL REALITY

AURORA WINTERS

CONTENTS

CHAPTER 1

Introduction

The Uncharted Potential of VR

Virtual reality (VR) technology holds a fascinating potential that continues to surprise us as it evolves, often exceeding the expectations set by previous display technologies. As we navigate through this innovative landscape, we are constantly discovering new applications and requirements that were previously unimaginable. Just as sports continuously evolve with new maneuvers and language expands with new expressions, the capabilities of VR are boundless, limited only by our imagination and individual circumstances.

The Advancement of Display Technology

As retinal display technology matures, more practical and mundane requirements, such as cost, come into play. The once daunting visi-computation challenges have been largely conquered, leading to a significant maturation of head-mounted displays (HMDs). Modern HMDs typically deliver at least full high-definition resolutions at sufficiently high refresh rates, ensuring a flicker-free and smooth visual experience. More significantly, future developments like the upcoming Oculus Rift Sonoma promise easy, passive stereo perspectives in head-tracked displays, further enhancing the immersive experience.

The Influence of Science Fiction

The concept of what we now refer to as virtual reality has long been a staple of science fiction, shaping our understanding and expectations of the technology. The Star Trek Holodeck, popularized over 30 years ago, serves as a prime example of how science fiction can inspire real-world technological advancements. Today, VR is an ever-expanding field, with practitioners and researchers continuously pushing the boundaries of what is possible.

Diverse Applications and Impressive Capabilities

Virtual Reality (VR) is a subject of ever-increasing enormity as practitioners and researchers inject more and more impressive capabilities into the technology. This special issue is devoted to exploring the extremes of the VR continuum—from fully synthetic immersive environments created by image-based rendering to largely synthetic environments for direct visualization of particle systems and truly "non-photorealistic" visualization of synthetic worlds.

CHAPTER 2

The History of Virtual Reality

Early Concepts and Foundations

The modern concept of "3D experiences" refers to computer-synthesized portrayals that place viewers within a simulated environment. This immersion is achieved through the integration of visual, auditory, and sometimes tactile feedback. Over the years, the term "cyberspace" has emerged, denoting a symbiotic universe where computing and virtual reality intersect. This concept, deeply rooted in science fiction, represents a digital realm interconnected with global data systems.

Science Fiction and Early Visionaries

The origins of virtual reality can be traced back to the influence of science fiction literature. Authors such as Vernor Vinge, William Gibson, and Kim Stanley Robinson pioneered the concept of cyberspace in their works. Vinge's "True Names" (1981), Gibson's "Neuromancer" (1984), and Robinson's novels about "virtual reality repairmen" introduced readers to the idea of immersive digital worlds. These works not only entertained but also inspired the technological advancements that followed.

The Emergence of Virtual Reality

By the mid-1980s, virtual reality had evolved into a unique domain of thought, development, and theoretical experimentation. This period marked the widespread adoption of the term "virtual reality" in both academic and popular discourse. The convergence of technological progress and the burgeoning internet played a pivotal role in shaping the VR landscape.

Morton Heilig and the Sensorama

The groundwork for virtual reality was laid even earlier, in the mid-20th century, by pioneers like Morton Heilig. Heilig's work focused on creating multisensory experiences, envisioning a future where viewers would feel as though they were part of the simulated scenario rather than merely watching it. Heilig's invention, the Sensorama, was a revolutionary device designed to engage multiple senses simultaneously. Described in the technical publication "Mechanical Simulation," the Sensorama featured a sensory convergence system that included visual, auditory, kinesthetic, and olfactory inputs.

Technological Evolution

As technology advanced, so did the potential applications of virtual reality. From its early days as a speculative concept in science fiction, VR has grown into a powerful tool for a wide range of uses, including education, entertainment, medical training, and beyond. The continuous development of VR technology has brought us closer to the immersive experiences once imagined in the pages of science fiction.

CHAPTER 3

Applications of Virtual Reality

The Ever-Expanding Frontier

The birth and development of VR as a novel and distinct form of experience stem from humanity's intrinsic curiosity and desire to create alternative worlds. We yearn to explore realms beyond our physical reality, driven by the need to experience, create, and benefit from new dimensions of existence. Today, VR represents a sector with virtually limitless possibilities, attracting substantial investments in research and development from individuals and institutions alike. The commitment to advancing VR is unwavering, with contributions ranging from specialized blogs and gaming websites to tech giants like Google and Samsung, who pour immense resources into enhancing VR hardware and software.

Diverse Applications and Immersive Experiences
Architecture and Design

In recent years, we have witnessed the rise of sophisticated virtual environments that simulate physical presence in both real and fictitious worlds. VR has revolutionized fields such as architecture and design. Imagine an architect tasked with designing a new hospital operating block. With VR devices, the architect can virtually walk through the space, identifying and addressing potential issues before construction begins. This immersive simulation allows for precise modifications and optimizations, ensuring a functional and efficient design.

Training and Education

VR's ability to create realistic and controlled environments makes it an invaluable tool for training in high-risk professions. Pilots, surgeons, astronauts, and firefighters, among others, can use VR to practice and hone their skills in simulated high-stakes scenarios without the associated risks. This not only improves their efficacy and safety but also enhances their preparedness for real-world challenges.

Therapeutic Applications

In the realm of healthcare, VR has found applications in therapy and rehabilitation. Patients undergoing therapy can immerse themselves in virtual environments that facilitate cognitive and emotional healing. For instance, VR can help patients confront and manage phobias, anxiety, and post-traumatic stress by gradually exposing them to controlled virtual scenarios. This approach fosters a change in their cognitive context, making it easier to process and overcome difficult sensations and events.

Entertainment and Gaming

The entertainment industry has been one of the biggest beneficiaries of VR technology. Gaming, in particular, has seen a revolution with the advent of VR. Players can now immerse themselves in richly detailed virtual worlds, experiencing games in a way that was previously unimaginable. VR gaming provides an unparalleled level of engagement, where players can interact with the game environment and characters as if they were physically present.

Education and Learning

Beyond professional training, VR is transforming educational experiences for students of all ages. Virtual field trips, historical recreations, and interactive science lessons are just a few examples of how VR can enhance learning. Students can explore ancient civilizations, dive into the depths of the ocean, or travel through the human body—all from the safety of their classroom or home. This immersive learning experience not only makes education more engaging but also helps students retain information more effectively.

Future Possibilities

As VR technology continues to evolve, we can expect even more innovative applications to emerge. The potential for VR to revolutionize industries and improve lives is immense. From virtual tourism and remote collaboration to advanced medical diagnostics and beyond, the future of VR promises to be as exciting as it is transformative.

CHAPTER 4

Advantages and Disadvantages of Virtual Reality

Defining Virtual Reality

Virtual reality (VR) is a synthetic environment created with computer graphics and accessed through specific devices. A good VR experience should embody three key characteristics:

- **Immersion**: The sensation of being physically present in a place other than the actual location.
- **Interactivity**: The ability for users to interact with the virtual world and for the virtual world to respond in real time.
- **Real-Time Environment Update**: The capability of the computers generating the virtual world to update the environment as the user's point of view changes.

Devices such as headsets and motion trackers are fundamental for this experience. Without them, the technology would merely be a 3D system rather than true virtual reality. This distinction is crucial because VR is built on the concept of creating immersive cyberworlds.

Advantages of Virtual Reality
Enhanced Learning and Training

One of the most significant advantages of VR is its application in education and training. VR can create realistic simulations that allow individuals to practice skills in a controlled environment. For example, pilots can train in virtual cockpits, surgeons can practice complex procedures, and students can explore historical sites or perform scientific experiments—all without the associated risks or costs of real-world training.

Immersive Entertainment

VR provides an unparalleled level of immersion in entertainment. Gaming, in particular, has been revolutionized by VR, offering players a chance to enter and interact with fantastical worlds. Beyond gaming, VR can be used for immersive movie experiences, virtual concerts, and interactive art installations, enriching the entertainment landscape.

Therapeutic Uses

In healthcare, VR is being used for therapeutic purposes. It can help patients manage pain, cope with anxiety, and recover from post-traumatic stress. By immersing patients in calming or controlled environments, VR therapy can facilitate mental health treatment and rehabilitation in ways that traditional methods cannot.

Remote Collaboration

VR enables remote collaboration by allowing people to meet in virtual spaces. This can be particularly useful for businesses with distributed teams, as it enables virtual meetings and collaborative work in a shared digital environment. This level of interaction can enhance communication and productivity, despite geographical distances.

Disadvantages of Virtual Reality
High Costs

One of the main drawbacks of VR is the high cost associated with the technology. High-quality VR headsets and compatible computers can be expensive, making it less accessible to the average consumer. Additionally, developing VR content requires significant investment in time and resources.

Health Concerns

Prolonged use of VR can lead to health issues such as eye strain, headaches, and motion sickness. These physical discomforts can limit the duration of VR sessions and hinder the overall user experience. Ensuring that VR experiences are designed with user comfort in mind is essential to mitigate these issues.

Limited Content

While the potential for VR is vast, the availability of high-quality content is still relatively limited. Developing VR content is complex and resource-intensive, which means that not all developers have the capacity to produce immersive and engaging VR experiences. This can result in a lack of diverse and high-quality content for users to explore.

Ethical and Privacy Concerns

The digital age has introduced new ethical complexities, especially in fields like VR. Issues such as data privacy, the digital divide, and the potential for addiction raise important ethical questions. Furthermore, the immersive nature of VR could blur the lines between virtual and real experiences, leading to potential psychological impacts.

Conclusion

Virtual reality offers a wealth of advantages, from enhanced learning and immersive entertainment to therapeutic applications and remote collaboration. However, these benefits come with challenges, including high costs, health concerns, limited content, and ethical considerations. As VR technology continues to evolve, it will be crucial to address these disadvantages to unlock its full potential and ensure it is used responsibly and ethically.

CHAPTER 5

Virtual Reality in Entertainment

The Fragmented Landscape of VR in Film

In the context of film, virtual reality (VR) is still a fragmented medium, with a noticeable gap between creators and audiences. Visionaries like Jorika Hendrickx are striving to bridge this gap and make VR more accessible through initiatives like the PLOF film and the PURO festival. These efforts highlight the intense and often chaotic nature of VR, revealing hidden truths through immersive experiences. Hendrickx, quoted by The Guardian in January 2017, captures the essence of VR's transformative potential: "The movement of our collective consciousness turns it upside down," as people find themselves deeply immersed in virtual environments that evoke profound emotional and physical responses.

Convincing Reality

Edge (2010) posits that the core objective of VR is to convince users of its reality. The immersive nature of VR aims to make the experience so convincing that users feel as though they are truly part of the virtual world. This sense of immersion can be so powerful that it challenges the boundaries between the virtual and the real, prompting users to question what they perceive.

VR and Augmented Reality in Entertainment

Virtual reality and augmented reality (AR) are transforming the entertainment industry by offering new ways for consumers to engage with content. Netflix, for instance, has expressed skepticism about VR's ability to surpass the traditional big screen and surround sound experience. However, both VR and Netflix are still in the early stages of their potential, and many aspects remain to be explored as technological and social barriers are addressed.

Obstacles to Adoption

Despite the excitement surrounding VR, several obstacles hinder its widespread adoption. Social and financial barriers play a significant role in limiting access to VR technology. For example, Nimo Zarkar, CEO of iDreamSky, noted a 40% decline in app downloads for entertainment and VR gaming apps. These challenges underscore the need for more affordable VR headsets and a broader range of compelling content.

The Future of VR Content

As the cost of VR headsets decreases, we can expect an increase in high-quality content that will attract more users. The entertainment industry is poised to embrace VR in new and innovative ways, from immersive gaming experiences and virtual concerts to interactive storytelling and beyond. The potential for VR to revolutionize entertainment is immense, promising to offer experiences that are not only visually stunning but also deeply engaging.

Conclusion

Virtual reality in entertainment is an evolving field with tremendous potential. While there are still significant challenges to overcome, the continuous advancements in VR technology and content creation will likely lead to a more integrated and immersive entertainment landscape. As we move forward, the gap between VR creators and audiences is expected to narrow, bringing us closer to a future where virtual experiences are an integral part of our everyday lives.

CHAPTER 6

Virtual Reality in Education

Immersive Learning Experiences

Virtual reality (VR) has revolutionized the way we approach education by providing immersive learning experiences that go beyond traditional methods. The Department of Quantum Science at the Australian National University (ANU) exemplifies this transformation. By using VR goggles, they offer students a near-death experience into a black hole. While reading Stephen Hawking's "A Brief History of Time" sparks curiosity, actually experiencing a simulated fall into a black hole elicits visceral reactions. Students confronted with the disorienting dimensions, instability, and rotation of nearby objects, and the deformation of the in-falling path due to the curvature of space-time, experience cognitive and emotional responses that classical education cannot provoke.

Enhanced Understanding Through Simulation

VR's ability to create interactive and engaging environments has been harnessed to develop museum and gallery tours, animated encyclopedias, and powerful tools for simulation and modeling. These tools are transforming the educational landscape, making it possible to explain complex concepts in chemistry, biology, physics, astronomy, engineering, and medicine in ways that were previously unimaginable. For example, secondary school physics students can now explore the intricate interactions between electrical fields, magnetic fields, motion, Maxwell's equations, the nature of radiation, electric charge, matter, time, and distance—all within a VR environment.

Emotional and Cognitive Impact

Understanding the pain and suffering of others can be challenging if one has never experienced similar situations. VR has the unique ability to simulate life-changing human experiences, providing empathy and deeper understanding. This was demonstrated at the ANU Open Day in 2018, where VR was used to mirror concepts taught in school, college, and university. By immersing students in realistic scenarios, VR helps them grasp complex and abstract ideas in a memorable and meaningful way.

Bridging the Gap Between Theory and Practice

One of the most significant advantages of VR in education is its ability to bridge the gap between theoretical knowledge and practical application. For instance, medical students can practice surgeries in a risk-free virtual environment before operating on real patients. Engineering students can design and test structures in VR, understanding the impact of various forces and conditions. This hands-on approach enhances learning outcomes and prepares students for real-world challenges.

Expanding Accessibility and Inclusivity

VR also has the potential to make education more accessible and inclusive. Students in remote or underfunded schools can access high-quality educational experiences that would otherwise be unavailable. Additionally, VR can accommodate various learning styles, making it possible for all students to engage with the material in ways that suit their individual needs.

Conclusion

Virtual reality is transforming education by providing immersive, interactive, and emotionally engaging learning experiences. From simulating complex scientific concepts to fostering empathy through realistic scenarios, VR is bridging the gap between theoretical knowledge and practical application. As VR technology continues to evolve, its potential to enhance education and make it more accessible and inclusive is boundless.

CHAPTER 7

Virtual Reality in Healthcare

Revolutionizing Healthcare Infrastructure

Virtual reality (VR) represents a significant advancement in healthcare infrastructure, offering an additional level of accessibility for both healthcare providers (HCPs) and patients. Future applications for health and wellness could integrate into this infrastructure, with new interactive, non-linear methods and algorithms advancing the participatory knowledge environment and democratizing information. This democratization involves traditional lens-based apps of immersion, home infusion, and facility-based care.

Treatment Support and Management

VR technology promises to revolutionize treatment support apps, integrating preventative and chronic management tools that assist in overall health and wellness. Achieving optimal system performance and integration compatibility with future health architecture requires innovative methodological and access approaches, addressed by developers and manufacturers.

Increasing Popularity Across Industries

VR is gaining traction in various industries such as aerospace, architecture, business, construction, education, film, historical recreation, economic development, and simulation. However, the healthcare industry is witnessing some of the most significant growth in immersive technology applications, impacting various aspects of patient care and provider operations.

Enhancing Patient Experience

For healthcare providers, VR applications can significantly enhance the quality of patient care. VR can provide support, improve access to treatment, and offer comfort and distraction during procedures. This leads to a better patient experience, which can result in substantial economic advantages for healthcare providers. Improved patient satisfaction can reduce the time required for certain treatments and enable earlier discharge, such as next-day releases.

Medical Training and Education

One of the most impactful applications of VR in healthcare is medical training and education. VR allows medical students and professionals to practice procedures and skills in a risk-free virtual environment. This hands-on training can improve proficiency and preparedness without the ethical and practical concerns associated with practicing on real patients. Surgeons can rehearse complex surgeries, and medical teams can simulate emergency scenarios to enhance coordination and response times.

Pain Management and Rehabilitation

VR is also proving effective in pain management and rehabilitation. Patients can be immersed in calming virtual environments during painful procedures, which can help reduce perceived pain and anxiety. VR-based physical therapy can make rehabilitation exercises more engaging and enjoyable, encouraging better patient compliance and outcomes.

Mental Health Treatment

In the realm of mental health, VR offers innovative treatment options for conditions such as anxiety, phobias, and post-traumatic stress disorder (PTSD). By exposing patients to controlled virtual scenarios, therapists can help them confront and manage their fears in a safe environment. VR therapy can also provide mindfulness and relaxation experiences, aiding in stress reduction and emotional well-being.

Telemedicine and Remote Consultations

As telemedicine continues to grow, VR can enhance remote consultations by creating immersive virtual meeting spaces. Patients and healthcare providers can interact in a more personal and engaging manner, improving communication and the overall consultation experience. VR can also enable remote monitoring and virtual home visits, making healthcare more accessible to patients in remote or underserved areas.

Conclusion

The application of virtual reality in healthcare is transforming the industry by enhancing patient experiences, improving training and education, and offering innovative treatment options. As VR technology continues to evolve, its integration into healthcare infrastructure promises to bring about significant improvements in patient care, accessibility, and overall health outcomes.

CHAPTER 8

Virtual Reality in Architecture and Design

The Evolution of Design Technology

With advancements in technology, especially in space exploration, the relationship between humans and their environment has transformed. Technical activities within these environments now involve sophisticated technology, from engineering design to construction. The increased role of computers in the design field has significantly impacted the growth and development of architectural forms.

Transition from Traditional to Computational Design

The shift from traditional manual model design to computer-based systems marked a new visual art principle. Initially, design evolved from two-dimensional to three-dimensional forms, leading to more complex and sophisticated results. This evolution continued with the development of computational design systems, moving from traditional models to intricate, algorithm-driven designs.

The Emergence of Virtual Architecture

One of the most significant advancements is the emergence of virtual architecture, where design transcends physical limitations. This new frontier allows architects to create and explore designs in digital and virtual worlds. The human mind may find it challenging to fully comprehend these complex designs because they exist beyond the tangible realm. Virtual reality (VR) provides the tools to dive into these digital environments, offering a new dimension of architectural exploration.

The Origins and Evolution of Architecture

Architecture began as a means of providing shelter, with the primary purpose of protecting people from natural forces and negative elements. Originally, it was functionally pragmatic, focusing solely on utility. As human civilization progressed, architecture evolved to encompass emotional and aesthetic dimensions. What started as simple shelters has transformed into complex artistic buildings, blending functionality with beauty.

Virtual Reality in Architectural Design

Virtual reality has revolutionized architectural design by offering immersive and interactive experiences. Architects can now create virtual models of their designs, allowing them to visualize and explore their projects in three dimensions. This immersive experience provides a deeper understanding of spatial relationships, proportions, and aesthetics.

Benefits of VR in Architecture

1. **Enhanced Visualization**: VR allows architects and clients to experience designs in a fully immersive environment, making it easier to comprehend and appreciate the final outcome.
2. **Improved Collaboration**: VR enables real-time collaboration between architects, designers, and clients, regardless of their physical locations. This fosters better communication and more efficient decision-making.
3. **Efficient Design Iteration**: Architects can quickly iterate and refine their designs based on feedback obtained from vir-

tual walkthroughs. This leads to better design outcomes and reduces the risk of costly modifications during construction.

4. **Client Engagement**: Clients can virtually explore their projects before construction begins, providing valuable insights and increasing their confidence in the design process.

The Future of Virtual Reality in Architecture

The potential for VR in architecture and design is immense. As technology continues to advance, we can expect even more innovative applications. Future developments may include augmented reality (AR) integration, where digital elements are overlaid onto the physical world, further enhancing the design and construction processes.

CHAPTER 9

Virtual Reality in Training and Simulation

The Origins of VR in Military Training

In 1985, the significant military VR simulator project STRICOM (Simulation, Training and Instrumentation Command) was initiated in Florida. STRICOM's employees focused on developing instructor training group training simulators, which provided exercises for a few operators supervised by an instructor. These simulators were designed to practice operating terminologies, maintain sustained attention, and foster teamwork in straightforward tasks. The military authorities have been major sponsors of the Soldier Cognition and Training group (SCAT) at the USAF Human Resource Lab. This organization is renowned for its cognitive task analysis, utilizing production rules with sets of conditions to guide actions from one course to another.

The Evolution of Military VR Applications

By the late 1990s, SCAT was engaged in developing advanced operator equipment, including laser weapons, integrated with VR helmet simulations. These advancements highlighted the military's commitment to leveraging VR technology to enhance training and operational readiness. The use of VR in military training allows for realistic, immersive simulations of combat scenarios, providing soldiers with valuable experience and preparation without the risks associated with live exercises.

Early Attempts and Educational Applications

The initial attempts to use VR technologies in education date back to the 1960s, preceding large-scale VR projects. In 1966, Ivan Sutherland created the "Sword of Damocles," a pioneering VR training device. The success of this concept led to the development of video-based flight simulators for pilots, marking the beginning of VR's application in training.

Support and Funding for VR Training

The idea of using VR technology for training was widely supported by military authorities. Their interest in new development areas, combined with the substantial improvement in combat capabilities through VR-based training, ensured consistent and robust funding for VR technology research. This support allowed for continuous advancements in VR training applications for military pilots, tank operators, and vessel captains.

Expanding VR Training Beyond the Military

While the military has been a major driver of VR training technology, its applications have expanded to various fields. VR training is now utilized in industries such as aviation, medicine, law enforcement, and emergency response. By providing realistic simulations, VR enables professionals to practice and refine their skills in a safe and controlled environment.

Aviation Training

In aviation, VR flight simulators provide pilots with immersive training experiences. These simulators replicate a wide range of flight conditions, emergency scenarios, and complex maneuvers, helping pilots build confidence and proficiency.

Medical Training

In the medical field, VR is used to train surgeons and medical personnel. VR surgical simulations allow practitioners to practice intricate procedures, improving their skills and reducing the risk of errors in real surgeries.

Law Enforcement and Emergency Response

Law enforcement officers and emergency responders use VR training to prepare for critical situations, such as hostage rescues, disaster response, and tactical operations. VR scenarios help these professionals develop decision-making skills and coordination under pressure.

Conclusion

Virtual reality has revolutionized training and simulation across various industries, providing realistic, immersive experiences that enhance learning and preparation. From its early applications in military training to its current use in aviation, medicine, law enforcement, and beyond, VR continues to transform how professionals train and develop their skills. As VR technology advances, its potential to improve training outcomes and operational readiness will only grow.

CHAPTER 10

Virtual Reality in Travel and Tourism

The Broad Potential of VR in the Travel Industry

Virtual reality (VR) is being explored in various sectors, and the travel and tourism industry is no exception. This industry involves diverse groups of people working together to create and add value to products and services. The potential of VR to enhance the travel experience is vast, and companies are starting to take the lead in utilizing this technology.

Early Stages of Development

Despite its promise, the application of VR in travel and tourism is still in its early stages. Essential infrastructure, such as hologram technology and investments in 5G, are necessary to fully develop VR capabilities. As VR technology continues to evolve and revolutionize the industry, travel companies will inevitably face challenges in adapting to these changes. However, the benefits are likely to outweigh the difficulties as VR becomes more integrated into travel experiences.

Enhancing the Guest Experience

With technological advancements, the guest experience has significantly improved. Travel destinations are finding creative ways to maintain competition and attract tourists. VR allows travelers to virtually visit desired locations before making travel decisions, offering a preview of what to expect. This technology can capture the interest of potential tourists and increase the visibility of travel destinations and brands.

Virtual Tours and Experiences

One of the most exciting applications of VR in travel is the ability to offer virtual tours and experiences. Travelers can explore famous landmarks, historical sites, and natural wonders from the comfort of their homes. This immersive experience provides a unique way to learn about various destinations and plan future trips. Virtual tours can also be beneficial for individuals who are unable to travel due to physical limitations or financial constraints.

Economic Impact

The global economy heavily relies on tourism. According to the Travel and Tourism Economic Impact 2018 report, travel and tourism contribute 8.3% of global GDP and are projected to provide 340 million jobs, accounting for 10.9% of total employment by 2028. The integration of VR in this industry has the potential to further boost economic growth by attracting more tourists and creating new job opportunities.

Future Possibilities

As VR technology continues to advance, the possibilities for its application in travel and tourism are endless. Future developments may include fully immersive travel experiences, where users can interact with virtual environments in real-time. This could revolutionize the way people explore new destinations, making travel more accessible and engaging.

CHAPTER 11

Virtual Reality in Social Interaction

Revolutionizing Online Dating and Social Connections
Virtual reality (VR) is transforming online dating by leveraging its immersive nature to bridge gaps in social interactions. This technology helps individuals connect and develop relationships more authentically, enabling millions to meet potential life partners in a genuine way. VR massively multiplayer online (VRMMO) platforms open new avenues for cultural exchange by allowing users to embody and interact through avatars, connecting in shared virtual spaces accessible via the Internet.

Enhancing Cross-Cultural Communication

VR provides the necessary infrastructure to facilitate socialization among individuals from different geographic locations, offering unique opportunities for cross-cultural communication. By recreating natural feedback and social interactions, VR stimulates genuine curiosity—essential for building trust and acceptance across diverse cultures. Access to virtual social worlds can help break down socioeconomic barriers, offering everyday experiences that reduce prejudice and stigma.

Addressing Social Interaction Difficulties

VR holds the potential to address various social interaction difficulties, such as shyness, social anxiety, and fear of public speaking. Research has shown statistically significant improvements in public speaking and non-verbal behaviors from using VR. Non-verbal behaviors, which constitute 65% to 95% of interpreted internal states and interpersonal perceptions, are crucial for effective communication. VR can enhance human sensitivity and accuracy in interactions, improving overall social skills.

High Fidelity VR Avatars and Social Presence

High fidelity VR avatar concepts are currently being pursued by many research teams, aiming to achieve compelling levels of social presence in VR. These avatars can create more realistic and engaging social interactions, making virtual environments feel more lifelike and personal.

Breaking Down Barriers

VR's ability to provide immersive experiences can help bridge social and economic gaps, creating inclusive social environments. By offering virtual experiences that simulate real-life interactions, VR can help individuals from different backgrounds connect and understand each other better, promoting inclusivity and reducing social stigmas.

Conclusion

Virtual reality is revolutionizing social interaction by enhancing online dating, facilitating cross-cultural communication, and addressing social interaction difficulties. As VR technology continues to advance, its potential to improve social connectivity and inclusivity is immense. With ongoing research and development, VR promises to create more realistic and engaging social experiences, breaking down barriers and fostering genuine human connections.

CHAPTER 12

Virtual Reality in Psychology and Therapy

Pedagogical and Research Applications

Virtual reality (VR) is a powerful tool for pedagogical and research purposes across various fields, including sports science, spatial memory, navigational abilities, visuospatial skills, and body representation. VR treatment allows users to navigate complex virtual environments and interact with synthetic objects from a first-person perspective, enhancing their sense of presence and engagement. This immersive experience promotes direct encounters with the phobic hierarchy, which can help reduce anxiety levels by creating credible conditions of presence in the virtual world. Just as in physical reality, the spatial properties and distances of observed objects in VR can influence anxiety levels, making the virtual world a credible and impactful tool for treatment.

Importance in Various Research Fields

Over the past 30 years, VR has become increasingly important in diverse research fields, including medicine, artistic education, history, archaeology, and cognitive psychology. VR is particularly valuable in curing psychological and neurological diseases, pain management, chronic pain treatment, and neuropsychological rehabilitation. By providing immersive and controlled environments, VR enables researchers to study and address complex psychological and neurological conditions more effectively.

VR-Based Exposure Treatments

VR-based exposure treatments have shown promising results for a range of conditions, including post-traumatic stress disorder (PTSD), panic disorder, agoraphobia, claustrophobia, acrophobia, and other clinically observed phobias, as well as some forms of obsessive-compulsive and conduct disorders. By repeatedly confronting fears and anxieties in a controlled virtual environment, VR treatment helps patients overcome avoidance mechanisms. This repeated exposure provides a therapeutic effect, as subjects in therapy feel a great sense of empowerment. The experiences in VR are often recalled as true experiences, rather than insubstantial imagination, leading to a decrease in emotional loads connected to their fears and anxieties.

Advancements in Cognitive and Behavioral Therapy

VR has revolutionized cognitive and behavioral therapy by offering new methods to treat psychological conditions. For example, VR can simulate public speaking scenarios to help individuals overcome social anxiety and fear of public speaking. By practicing in a virtual environment, patients can build confidence and improve their performance in real-life situations. Similarly, VR can create safe and controlled environments for treating various phobias, allowing patients to face their fears gradually and systematically.

Pain Management and Rehabilitation

In addition to psychological treatment, VR is also used for pain management and physical rehabilitation. Immersive VR experiences can distract patients from pain during medical procedures, reducing their perceived pain levels. VR-based physical therapy exercises can be more engaging and enjoyable, encouraging better patient compliance and improving rehabilitation outcomes.

Future Prospects and Ethical Considerations

As VR technology continues to evolve, its applications in psychology and therapy are expected to expand further. However, it is important to consider ethical implications, such as ensuring patient privacy and maintaining the authenticity of the therapeutic experience. Researchers and practitioners must balance the benefits of VR with ethical considerations to ensure its responsible and effective use.

Conclusion

Virtual reality has transformed the fields of psychology and therapy by providing immersive, interactive, and effective treatment options. From addressing phobias and social anxieties to managing pain and aiding rehabilitation, VR offers a versatile and impactful tool for improving mental health and well-being. As technology advances, VR's potential to enhance therapeutic outcomes will continue to grow, promising a brighter future for psychological and therapeutic interventions.

CHAPTER 13

Virtual Reality and Ethical Considerations

Historical Roots of Ethical Considerations in Simulations
Ethical considerations in multi-user simulations have deep historical roots. The first military simulation efforts, such as Ernst Udet's celluloid biplane models during the First World War, set the stage for later ethical reflections. Udet, a German general, faced the consequences of his leadership decisions at the Nuremberg trials and ultimately chose suicide under unknown circumstances. While the ethical implications of these early simulations were significant, they did not reach the scale of the existential quandaries faced by creators and users of modern multi-user, responsive, immersive technology.

The Intersection of Theater and Simulation Ethics

The extensive history of theater as a foundational player in exploring ethics forms the cornerstone of today's cultural suppositions. However, the realities of responsive simulations, which are central to emerging virtual experiences, have not been extensively communicated through a broad and rigorous scrutiny of ethical considerations. As virtual reality (VR) continues to develop, it is crucial to address the ethical implications of these immersive technologies.

Opportunities and Challenges of Information Technology

Advances in information technology present both opportunities and challenges. As society grapples with the consequences of increasingly sophisticated and pervasive digital simulations and systems, thoughtful analysis is required to understand the impact on individuals and societies. Virtual worlds contribute to knowledge, communication, research, commerce, culture, and human development. They are embedded within our civic society, legal systems, economies, networks, and media.

The Role of VR in Daily Life

The generation of children who will become adults in 2025 will grow up in a world where computer-mediated and artificial sensory information is an integral part of their daily experiences. As such, it is essential for competent communities and insightful global leaders to navigate the complex interfaces between policy and technological advances. Policymakers need to address these issues with careful attention, ensuring that ethical considerations are at the forefront of technological development.

Ethical Challenges and Considerations

Privacy and Data Security

One of the primary ethical concerns in VR is the issue of privacy and data security. VR systems collect vast amounts of personal data, including biometric information, which can be sensitive and susceptible to misuse. Ensuring robust data protection measures and transparent data usage policies is critical to safeguarding user privacy.

Consent and Manipulation

In VR environments, the line between reality and simulation can blur, raising concerns about informed consent and manipulation. Users must be fully aware of the extent of their engagement with VR and the potential impact on their psychological and emotional well-being. Transparent communication and ethical design practices are essential to prevent manipulation and ensure user consent.

Digital Divide and Accessibility

The proliferation of VR technology can exacerbate the digital divide, creating disparities in access to immersive experiences. Ensuring equitable access to VR technology and addressing socioeconomic barriers is crucial to prevent further marginalization of underserved communities.

Psychological and Social Impact

The immersive nature of VR can have profound psychological and social effects on users. Prolonged exposure to virtual environments may lead to issues such as addiction, desensitization, and altered perceptions of reality. Ethical considerations must include the potential long-term impact on mental health and social behavior.

Conclusion

As virtual reality technology continues to evolve, it is imperative to address the ethical considerations that come with its development and use. From privacy and consent to accessibility and psychological impact, a thoughtful and comprehensive approach is required to navigate the ethical landscape of VR. By prioritizing ethical considerations, we can ensure that the benefits of VR are realized while minimizing potential harm and promoting a responsible and equitable digital future.

CHAPTER 14

Challenges and Future Developments in Virtual Real

The Quest for True Presence

One of the most pressing challenges in VR technology is establishing a true sense of presence. Presence is the feeling that a user genuinely exists within the virtual environment and is an integral part of it. This sensation is crucial for studying the psychological and physical effects of VR on various aspects of human behavior, cognition, and imagination. These include the development of the human brain, social use laws, environmental beliefs, learning, mood, and physical recovery from trauma, such as clinical treatments. Achieving true presence involves improving real-time rendering, processing capabilities, lighting, audio, haptics, locomotion, and avatars.

Mixed Reality Spaces

The development of mixed spaces, where virtual and augmented reality (AR) converge, is essential to overcoming current VR/AR setup issues. These include auditor tracking, space invasions, and health and safety guidelines. A strategic objective is to design these mixed spaces to enhance user experiences while maintaining safety and comfort. This involves abandoning the concept of authenticity in an electronically-mediated world and embracing the evolution of human interaction through in-depth gaming experiences, both real and unreal. These experiences can lead to introspective healing and a deeper understanding of humanity.

Addressing User Comfort and Health

VR systems can cause discomfort in users, such as eyestrain and nausea, particularly if the systems are not optimized for user comfort. To address these issues, advancements in eye tracking, foveation (reducing the rendering burden on peripheral vision), and improvements in latency and frame refresh rates are essential. These features can enhance realism and mitigate medical issues associated with VR head-mounted displays (HMDs). Additionally, enabling users to control, display, and share VR experiences on multiple connected screens can broaden the accessibility and appeal of VR.

Ethical and Philosophical Reflections

The philosophical consequences of VR technology are profound, prompting reflections on the nature of human experience and cognitive self-enrichment. The goal is not only to understand our systems of thought but to cherish them through extensive reflections on how VR can influence consciousness and behavior. This reasoning extends beyond VR to the observation of reality itself, emphasizing the importance of perception and psychological flexibility in understanding human experience.

Technological Advancements and Integration

VR and AR are among the most exciting directions in science and technology today. VR has opened new paradigms of experimental design and research tools in neuroscience and psychology. However, the practicalities of understanding phenomena such as global citizen science and customization also benefit from VR's capabilities. The ongoing developments in VR technology, including better processing power, more realistic simulations, and improved user interfaces, will continue to push the boundaries of what is possible.

Conclusion

The fields of VR and AR present both significant challenges and immense opportunities for future development. Addressing issues of presence, user comfort, and ethical considerations are crucial to advancing the technology. As VR continues to evolve, it holds the promise of transforming various aspects of human life, from education and training to social interactions and entertainment. By focusing on these challenges and embracing innovative solutions, we can unlock the full potential of VR and create a more immersive, inclusive, and enriching virtual future.

CHAPTER 15

Conclusion

Rekindled Interest and Multidisciplinary Applications
Virtual reality (VR) has rekindled interest among scholars, researchers, and practitioners, marking a new frontier in human experience. The general implications of new VR technologies extend across a wide range of multidisciplinary applications, including cultural heritage, training, innovative communications, entertainment, and addressing social and health pathologies with dramatic clinical conditions. In our increasingly interconnected world, where specialization in work is balanced with diverse social interactions and education in heterogeneous groups, VR tools play a crucial role in providing cohesive and authentic interpretations of the new challenges faced by humanity.

Leveraging VR's Potential
Despite the extensive media coverage and hype surrounding VR, the true potential of this technology can only be realized through careful and critical use in specific scenarios. VR is a promising medium at the dawn of the 21st century, but its applications must be interpreted with a historical perspective to maintain their relevance and impact. This approach will open new dimensions for exploring human experience, guided by curiosity and a desire for understanding.

Technological Developments and Enhanced Experiences

Interest in VR, which waned during the last two decades of the twentieth century, has been reignited by recent technological advancements. These developments have enabled more immersive and natural interaction modes, significantly enhancing the sense of presence and enjoyment of VR applications. However, the initial promises of VR may have faded due to unrealistic expectations that VR would be "magic" and inherently wonderful once developed. Like other cultural and communication media, VR carries cultural and technological "baggage" that must be leveraged thoughtfully.

Critical Stance and Ethical Considerations

Producers and users of VR must adopt a critical stance, recognizing the cultural and technological context of the medium. Focusing solely on market potential and economic gain without considering the broader implications risks creating a "Frankenstein" experience. It is essential to remember that in literature, Dr. Frankenstein was the creator of the monster, not the monster itself. This metaphor underscores the importance of responsible and ethical development and use of VR technology.

The Future of VR

In conclusion, VR is a more than promising medium that offers vast possibilities for enhancing human experience. Its applications in various fields, if approached with historical perspective and critical insight, can lead to a joyful and wide-ranging exploration of human potential. As we move forward, it is vital to keep applications in their proper dimension, ensuring that VR serves as a tool for enriching and understanding human life rather than becoming an unchecked technological force.